N

Far-Dale

Dennis Barone

NAUSET PRESS

WAREHAM, MASSACHUSETTS

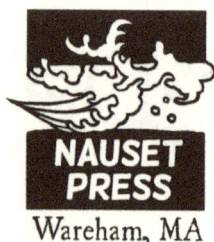

NAUSET PRESS

Wareham, MA

Book and Cover design by Nauset Press

Cover Art: Fragment of the painting *Blue Horizon*, 2020 by April
Gornik. With permission of the artist. See the full artwork at:
www.aprilgornik.com/artwork/2011-2020

Published by Nauset Press, LLC
Publishing contact: info@nausetpress.com

ISBN-13: 978-1-962890-09-0
Library of Congress number pending

For Debbie

Contents

New Poems

POND AND OCEAN

Now we dream back no longer what's up
next. Still each new day we step on
a path, beyond an entrance, greeted in friendship.
An open gate, each person swinging;
saying, "howdy."

Red Dress, Gray Suit, Brown Squirrel. No
complaints, disguise, or violence.
Marsh-hawk, conjure these trees global
umbrella and make its measure infinite.
Rose blossoms become duvet.

Although so many historians say no future now;
although one and a half million walkers killed by firearms;
instead, early in mornings heritage roses release a kiss.
Now believe apocalypse an ancient mistake.
Tie shoes left over right, etc., and proceed.

Here's a carousel, a see-saw and
one remarkable razzle that has lines
waiting patiently and kindly and each
greets the other one-hundred languages;
none, misunderstood.

So, we'll take this, export it, require
that spore-like effort spreads to
relinquish "I" and gather together as
"we" here, now in the park.
Hello, friends.

Multiple birds, one stone.

LIGHTS LEFT ON

I still see them some nights;
that troubles me.
What are they asking?

If we could walk again
where something would be purchased.
The department of departed ones —

haunt me or hurry me
to where the wakeful attend.
What is it that parents ask?

You too my son they seem
to say can do something
good if not a thing miraculous.

The boy who walks does not
fly: walks and glad-hands and
has memories of getting there.

Bless little shivering bird-like things.

THE SPHERE

We met meek and lowly
Abrupt action under our call

He will trust a particular veil
Pathetic chapter added in reward

What free and easy book drawn
Hospitable country first contrived

With days the strangest fortress
Published key to the sorrowing

His character innocent but
Antiquated and bitter miles

We enter publicly the stronghold
Dedicated to evenings real, original

His confession torn of doubt
Ashamed, lost time as well

He assured direct passage
Considered service no measure

He tells the deepest sentence
Permitted comfort during profession

She surpassed the necessity
Enabled a particular here and now

Yes, marble from the snow
Adorned a true attraction

And shone as the diamond all need

WORK

A brush, a clumsy grizzly
wall of mirrors, a euphemism.
A baking sheet repeated with pride.
A pickaxe lifted, a shovel whose
luxury left town.
A chisel, a bulldozer and now
a page — tall grass,
modern conveniences and
a world shed.

DOUBLE OR NOTHING

Comfort car watched a limp
one of the game all-day rock
and a little bit yes, yes

Stepped closer to remove lucky
man lay back in those maybe
you get then removed it

His head slowly muffin skip
forget go back echoes you think
hung up and placed like that?

Red face didn't he tell you
yes and no a glass to beat it
he seems sounds right arm

Neighborhood kids up first smiling
apologizing when in response
about tonight the cold black curve

Dressed three times the second that story
then topped-off again thinking
in the midst of the music

Hello, out to listen and have
supper oh have supper why
don't you high whine some guilt

Lamplight floating into air
the morning left with the milkman
it means don't go downtown

You mean even the game the room

a beast of burden you got little
clubs best of all a piece

Picture the luncheonette its replica
and faking the fools, thousands
a pain to the bus stop

Relax words and knowing
the matter placed in arms
now filled up with eyes open

Sometimes most of the time
to take it the smell the voice
pleasant and beside their play

Paced and watched it
the mirror into our house
cash from the luncheonette

Across the street at the hotel
shook concern saucers plates
could not stop shaking it

Nothing nice and cool a new
mix a calm return a nod
and would see them be better

Then moved like a key in the
living room trying to forget
run smooth into the medicine

Troubadour in a tower kept after
one thing to suggest the house
more than the rest of them

What's so sad dusty streets
real and unreal from remembered
days and sunk into a hole

Flush the money opposed
foldaway desires the bank
the muscles the sneakers

Glass doors on the sharp
with anger not here and now
folded luck they had buying

A shave ordered scrambled
eggs until calm and kissed
by a chair like swollen this

One matter for the machine
the sales the next day the
only one but don't worry

This house icy feelings and
let the worry mark my words
against the wall brown earth

Air-conditioned time coming
and days like vacations
but they reached all that

House back with property those
keys clean shirts like a person
along the highway to a settled

Place the front row the pillow
the stuff of life things freaky
crazy cash for the night

SALT

A design like success,
hardly in this city despite
the purchase and celebration.

A Doric column marked
at the same stonewall,
same large window.

A boom and bust —
the western edge reminds
creatures to scheme,

a faux design, fake
like a joint purchaser
drifting into the center.

A red light included,
things due in the wide-
ranging success or fame.

A silence like another out
for it jaded because
who answered at a whim:

a system unconscious,
an unsafe place, unpacked
and unwanted at night.

A remarkable double-sided
banner fronts the contemporary
in this bright homeland.

But snippets and years
of interest will return across
Wolcott, Wallingford and Winsted.

An imagined portrait, a
difficult poem, a tease,
a plum pocket nostril vac.

So, there's the essence,
the money, calm utility
and ultimate hand-off.

A force right now,
not a warm personality,
the gathered: Kevin, Elaine.

A LOST STORY

A husband and wife.
He cooked at an officers' mess.
She ... not remembered.
They had a dog and
a small house.
They often went fishing
and tied their own
lures. He put up
with a lot where he
worked and once an
officer called him out
from the kitchen to
meet a senator. He
found it unpleasant,
offensive and later
that day went home
and took the dog
for a walk. The
little dog's name
... not remembered.

FAR-DALE

Words to bless the flight, encouraging
words upon arrival, for greeting and
directing to the next phase, a hotel of sorts
or a neighborhood.
Words that hide the truth and others
that reveal it — setting out, then
pulling back the door.
Words misspelled or illegible, discounted
and taken aback by the interest rate.
Carnivalesque words and an ordinary
day or drumbeat sound like a beat
at the end of sounds not spoken,
a tap and rounded out by a toast
to tomorrow because the other day . . .

Might light have an action
of embarrassed experience?
There would be a spirit flame if
the frame could hold it.
There would be one answer to
all your questions, if tied
to participate. At the intersection
where variables meet, resolution
might hold a brilliant moon
that does wait for the speaker
to speak something previously
heard: directions.
Update: you think —
wild in shape.
You see a tower, but
it's not there, see cats

cry in the light. A nail
through a word hammered
into a wall. One window
shut and nothing to be seen.
That word rendered illegible
by the nail.

You need words to impart this emotion:
on the road   in the office
back home   on the mountain-top
off-shore.   Yodel by the window.
Yodel on the sofa   because
it is pleasing to do so,
especially in the top-floor
dark where the turn must be
inside since you can't see outside.
Out the window all that is
unspoken and dark.

EVERYTHING SILENT

Column, no border.
Through wing, sleep
around dew from travel.
Grasp this spur, this
groove that whispered
its stop. Ready to
right water when
it shifts in swirls,
wind. Harbor there
the map not found,
the taken away and
the words for rain.
Here among reckless
assurance, worried
no price out of reach.
It will last once
everything steps on this
street, stretches here
on stone. Break
out as rain bringing
stanzas to breathe,
spell out a sample
off dusty peaks
and bright descent.

WALK WITH A WEIGHT

There are no words —
shadow to the ground
sometimes empty, hidden
or expected and away.

There are no words —
each like all by day
fallen tatters, particles
that sound a hesitation.

There are no words —
reborn only pantomime
of reality warmed and
every so often possible.

There are no words —
neither the contrary nor
a change into silence
leaves us the trunk of things.

There are no words —
waking the dream or
everything abandoned to
muttering doubt.

There are no words —
seeing is center always
what doesn't exist
walk with a weight

held low in one hand;

turn, then walk with
it held high over your
head.

BACKWARDS

Hoping is for many
individuals buried thanks to
falling and its oblivion.

Inevitability is not born
in braggadocio for sentimental
hurting like our thought.

Present mind must silence
an error like a probe in
dryness forgotten too much.

Functions pond these stories,
the teeth above a tune's perspective
that gives a wrench its full.

Vision wanted. Bust a slide,
cut inept thread, speed
hammers about cramped spinning.

Slipper-manage what happens
and turn all paths today — oh,
maker get the meantime.

Memory follows endless stuff
grating a name, believing
activity fits around policy.

Ring, ring — you won't plan,
sing, fault or flame.

MAQUETTE

the stillness of objects, of
sounds, sailboats, and
dancers

Three felt moved, always
cold. These things protect
home.

Marks of town slipped
each thought so busy in
linen fix and risk.

Richard said: loneliness —
"a simultaneous feeling of
immediacy and distance."

That arsenal of rain
turned back to either
life. Sheaf clear.

Leaves blamed for
unraveling questions and
what morning

lines with labor, with
soul. Absolutely deep,
hard weight.

Nothing is ...

Okay, that's even
obligatory and what looks
really used.

Something beat inside
well-lit verse, still
trailing premonition.

Then distant ghosts
going bone-book up ...
dangerous work.

WISHFUL THINKING

When you get off the interstate
take Mrytle to Main. You'll save
half-a-mile.

That's the sort of advice
I can give you about Plainville,
the town where I live.

You don't need GPS or a map.
Just ask me. But tomorrow
I have an appointment

at a Medical Center in the
Capital City. I get lost there,
can't figure it out —

north or south. Who laid it
out? I wonder. I may not
like what I'm told.

Here in town we have a grid;
in the city, a labyrinth. Too
many twists

and turns. Too many questions.
Too few answers. Parking
is never free,

either in town or city. And so
I find it's best to stay home
and watch the TV.

I can tell you everything
that's on every channel—
as well as

how to get from here to
there.

MONKEY MAN

Here's where the horse fell.
Wires and ropes kept the clearing
safe for us, not so for the horse.

We ran for adventure, not shelter,
past the pool and an improvised
long jump pit. Who survived

and for how long? It could be
seconds after the attack or decades.
With additives we might mark

moments of metamorphosis. I can
send a message but it will not
explain our title. On this date:

forge an emotional connection
with your audience

Not one, not two, but three
cars went through the red-light
and walk sign.

I almost stepped into the street.

When turning on red look left
look right look left again.
Speed bumps for speeding cars.

We are working on it.
Be safe.

DON'T FORGET YOUR LOCATION

A contradiction described as
an egg. At first the picture
revealed fixed stars, great lakes,

and the sites about to break
old facial expressions. The opening
scene unknown and

bid to abundance. Yanked
abroad as if swept from
dress. Always a well.

After sunset its full
gaze thought to be slightly
captain and absolute.

Deficiency occurred across
mythologies. A slap carried
off natural habit

as a later story version
around the eyes and a little
peace on earth.

A table that features its
height with regards to advantage.
One day anticipation

produced circumstances and
sounds. Astrological map,
this map as the other

eye to dispel such music
as out the petals. Avail
that measure the red-yellow

glow. As particular as
colors constituted a bright
glow in the channels

of cloud puckered spirits.
A complementary table or
chair made of paper

placed with respect to
a map and perspective
still to bridge. Numerous

antiquaries gave once more
help, a solution made with
salt and glue.

THOROUGHFARE

Walker's corral has no horses
in it. Like the ponds of paradise,
it has been emptied out, filled
in, and built up, but not for
silver or gold, rather, something
concrete and basement-like; yet,
some thought the place
to begin would have been orbital,
so far from our old Main Street and
its narrow limits.

How close pest must be to poet
or the dancer that ran a musical
for those who aspired to exit town
pool, old grammar school—
holding tight in hand all swag
that offered such immense swagger
about town: ten-speed, high-top sneakers,
tie-pin, and ring. Then jumped
off the hood of a parked Duster and
into someone's outstretched arms.

From boundary to boundary those high
walls collapsed into the deep end.
It used to seem limitless, a hike
through zones of flowers and weeds.
It used to increase width, length,
and success so valiant were its
garages. Now, even Mayor Worthy
wants his retirement far from such
diminished falls and attractions. Curbside,

he found a dime and brought it home.

Founders' Day arrives. Mayor Worthy
sleeps late; Dr. Walker attends cats
and dogs. First, the Scouts go by
and then the teams, so many of them
and yet so few compared to prior
eras. Night arrives and no one
haunts cemeteries or woods. What
heritage we have has been passed over
and under so that we know our tradition as
one to which no one else subscribes.

Found and lost? Well, imagine Corvettes—
affluence—latest fashion; in short,
money. Torn down: Shop-Rite and
grammar school; Lyons Service Station
and that grand Tower of Pizza. Valentine
Creek trapped in a culvert, tapped for
nothing. The crayfish dried and died out.
Something shines bright at one streetlight.
Something reminds me that it used to be
home and this home, a house of wonder.

ROMANCE

Life in a crescent
lit by a quarter-moon

unseen. Some stay
flesh-like, others mimic

stone. Images hide words
as if white arrows

black tar has covered.

from After Math

STAY WITH US

The house is not built,
not even begun.
This house is a cloud,
this bliss of stars,
a princox of evening:

June evening, a green
evening sighted as if
young and without any
scent or shade. This
house half-dissolved in
evening.

SIDE-STRADDLE HOP

if beauty is as beauty does
you'd break open a dictionary just to watch
the words pour out
    —Barry Schwabsky

Sigh Arnold — it could be worse
such windows need caulking and then
nothing from outside, not even a protest
or campaign to limit building heights.

It was years before hugging became an
accepted practice in Kansas. Yet, the North
Cemetery has more names than one
can guess though few make an attempt.

If then the measurements do not align
at least find a memorable name;
perhaps not Arnold but rather Ziggy
Duke of Camphor and Vice-Regent Supreme.

We read all correspondence backwards
and forwards smack into Kingdom Come
regretting that Lisa had redacted most
dates. My cheese blend, please.

How ordinary the command to inflect
or replace your balloon at the Max Bar
or somewhere uptown such heartfelt
timber for the flames of another birthday.

Out weaving want into give for
heaven's sake, please guard your gold
like answers to the final exam or

our playbook's burnished plans.

In an exact reenactment except one
farb wrecks it with impossible shoelaces
and a lemon lollipop placed horizontal be-
tween two fingers where the weapon belonged.

Between inaccuracies and precision,
dominion everywhere granted to the infected fly
desperate to turn midflight and instill
contagion deep into the cantankerous filament.

The soldier coshed an inspector general,
a matter of class, of the will to define terms;
to suggest and not to name. Or was it
broom flower on imagined Tuscan hills?

The wish to enter this palace or to
create whether barred or embraced,
to recall red paint before government and
abandoned, reckless and wild along the bulwark.

The ornate ticket beyond all possibility of
merger with either shrimp or escarpment
begs for attendant color. My friend, please
pick up your packages soon.

The amoeba shops in small sizes and
wants many pairs but no earmuffs
this year charted for grandiose accumulation:
rupture an anchor and each cell drifts seaward.

Serve our senior an S-curve. Why not
commiserate: an offer of platitudes memorable
and listed, no dictum not said to

each correspondent given a nickel's sense.

If Arnold met G-Men at the Mizpah Hut to
declare chiaroscuro the way of the world,
would the old man return to this hillside
scowling once more at lit Jack-O-Lanterns?

The count is one, two, three; not
one and two and three and ... Stasis,
somewhere between ancestor and descendant.
Side-straddle hop. Side-straddle hop. One and

shall we begin. Ready, set — commence.
It would have been enough: oggi qui;
domani là, ma sempre la musica.
What can I possibly say, huh?

An atmospheric portal or parlor — think
about such things, a shift of syllables
that confuses messages and messengers,
managers and management of two books.

Ah, brief radiance creased, sotted,
foiled and tinged; notwithstanding one's
ardor for reflection and hypothesis, the scientific
method tied up with yellow ribbons and bows.

She must have known more titles or,
at least, one title of more words,
disturbing syllables shortened to make
sour sounds sweet even if incorrect.

The faith we placed in academics — both
subjects and souls — had been misplaced.
Arnold had no answers and refused to

ask questions of himself, of us.

The gold-plate method guaranteed signs,
ritual phrases meant for alarm and
satisfaction as if sculpture brought with it
an ideal speculation equal to a solid object.

A luminescence perhaps that hid rather than
illumined, something that G-Men figured, if
removed, might reveal one plot or another,
something, as they say, hidden in plain sight.

From order to mess; from walk to bridge,
so many fragrant steps turned to so
few. South side of an avenue in need
for pride of place and a new name.

This badge, this blade; this help, this
held commemoration for bridgework
and repaving interiors, not just facades.
Shut down or sign out. Exfoliate.

In exact measure, the poetry, the not always
yesterday, the God of it, everything, music,
image from between the light and the dark,
one sigh, John, one song and one sigh.

The morning, the window, the wrong suffered,
those words, a belief passing through that instant,
affirmed — if you look: how, what, what (again)
is without acquaintance affirmed.

A turn sign of erupting remarkable for
miracle, story ever-changing, a place
for everyone to sit down and be present

and here and say, sing, sigh, and sign.

Poetry decides power, not politics
or wealth, not torment. Fierce company,
those ragged lines, spells of a magician
that become; over time, more curse than elixir.

For compensation, decorative gold non-
refundable rattle, dry worms and G-Men.
Yes, but Arnold composed a sequence
in delay, familiar, but rarely sacrosanct.

A sufficient equipoise, a tangible balance
that is anti-aphoristic, that is economy
in scale, free-flowing tar-scape,
scraped and shuttered, silenced and sealed.

Men sigh. Between determined bounds,
light so threatened exchange that
our lives predicted return and
then all premonition turned to soot.

The toot-toot of our tug taught others
an approach initiated — always —
comradery, an utterance offered as balm
and comfort, an opening for light.

Yesterday, sincerely yours and tomorrow
exquisite jubilation renewed and brilliant.
The stride — if shortened, just quicken it.
Maintain the pace; please these feet.

The pleasure embraced, but the embrace itself
surely not the only pleasure possible here,
not with that light nor this taste on the tongue

so soon after crossing the lips' threshold.

Not the crime nor the criminal, not the
math of the mathematician but the painter's
blue and the composer's clef and the poet's
pause at the edge of Kaaterskill Falls.

Always sublime, yes, but its definition
changes even if the word stays the same:
spelling; pronunciation. Look at that
window and then look through it.

An ecstasy, praise no longer partitioned.
God stutter on the street and marvelous
there caught in the air everything effluent,
incantation that ameliorates and then illumines.

It conjures John, this misnomer embraced
by Arnold as commemoration of the gold-
plated everything configured and
commemorated no matter how tiny or wise.

Not taken for granted but taken nonetheless;
with our friend, together, hands waving.
Encore. Encore of joy. An
utterance poured out across tablets.

Everything befriended and embraced, even
the spider and the snake. Be embraced G-Men,
no visage to be greeted with drawn weapon.
Enter the tulip pattern — don't straddle

the walkway. Hop on. Breathe. Green and
yellow. How does the song begin?
Music for John and the G-Men and every-

body dancing so happy, happy that

it conjures day out of night. Someone
else gladdens at this instance, reaches for
all gathered by the river, joins them, eight
of them bathed by the Ofanto's slow waters.

Union, loose union. Warmed-up. Ready
to run for fun like the Striders. We are
ready. Limber. Words do pour out and
when we touch them, they flame.

POCKET CHANGE

Paramus won't last
as long as Paradise.
Hide between words
a difficult world.
What we explore
must revisit mourning
and those details of
particular incidents;
desires thwarted.
The street became
crowded with people,
no goats came forth.
Bells rang in the souls
of strangers. One
brought refreshments and
sat while others talked
of the gospel. What
wrath is against us!
What a change has
come! Quick as that—
our refuge, a poolroom
now a mission. There
was much singing and
no reproach: justice
and righteousness and
civilities of an evening.

GIFTS

In the window
the sun would not stay.
The only thing
earned, a name. It
was lost, abandoned
perhaps out of respect.
What happens,
probably won't to you.
A hole in paper,
a sad inheritance like
another life taped
to a mirror. There's
nothing in this standing
place. Gulls go home,
not even the memory
of things. As if in the
past and yet back and forth,
the unfeasible plan for
another season. Still
something intended—
a line of tracks
crossed and another one
sent. In sight, the kitchen
and staying on the ground,
happy in the photograph.

NO MEN OF GRACE

All five had walked into a bar
on Carmine Street: three Montagues
and two Capulets. No need to

guess what happened. A fight
broke out and somehow all five
got themselves killed. In their

likenesses one sees their skulls
shorn of hazel skin. Boaz says
long-headed Italians become round

headed after a single generation
on Manhattan Island. Study the skulls,
Professor. Environment will not

displace inherited traits. These
Italians had demonstrated their
proficiency with the knife.

They are by nature this way
and no other. Titian, the artist,
likewise: study his etchings,

their fine cut lines; yet
distrust so idolatrous a scheme:
this beauty paid for in blood.

WAVE RIDER

secrets of ourselves and
sausage, egg, oil, and
split-level owned private
furniture at once seduced and
remote passport is what the
and I told myself the rules art
and downtown insisted, chosen
and radiant I understood one
point sure of merit shows and
see that contaminated legend and
my hidden village for fifty years
and be careful Coca-Cola exile
and tissue comedy a local
ingredient trying to remember and
love come dinnertime perhaps
and spent the day honest accident
and other problems next door
an overarching philosophy a
different kind of furious a
solid living a key a classic
tale and haunting money
bemused indecision a man like
a buffer a mark of idols and
my work continued I spoke of
axes abroad good health the city
center old laboriousness and sometimes
sweaters old tires
powerful men change and
social inertia suddenly I
believed all over this day
beauty and hand in hand

Botticelli shock to cushion
cypresses sepulchers and nostalgia

PURÉE

Share the use of a comma
Sharpen a pen and
Disguise the mannequin, the
Protagonist at whim or
At wheel and dial back
That number extend
Extend the limit eliminate
Limitations take no
For your answer budget
Spending with discretion
Hold down the number
Praise each committee's
Work hold down the number
Dial again and
Look up the answer
Look up the disguise
Identify the markings
Deer skin or hawk wing
No winter snow
Insurance for skiers
A harbor-stitch saves
Nine

Avoid the house   faded in the night
None may choose   blizzard in the
How much money   take me home
Take the sand   an area of land
Perception of words   another hey hey
Blue sea laughing   links on a chain
A hard road
Nobody home

from A Field Guide to the Rehearsal

HOLD STILL

That any eye may see it: the drift of a ship mid-sea or line. And what comes up from the ground this time of year: anticipated, but not yet green.

COPIOUS NOTES

Three pages. Now counting. A shopping-list. A to do list. Too many for that. Think of the mat alongside the frame, the crosswalk, or something hung on the refrigerator. A full roll of paper towel, no printed design applied. Agnes Martin very early in the morning. Wallace Stevens in winter. A coffee mug with no coffee; a teacup with no tea. Something sanitized before surgery. A thick book looked at from the side, someone's autobiography. Fog—when the car lights hit it just so (now we're moving). Robert Irwin alone in his room. Someone's eyes closed, ready for yoga-practice or prayer. Morris's empty loom. Carrara or "oh, moon," etc. Fifty-year old appliances: still working. Lampshades or drum-skins. The dots of polka-dots. A lightbulb lit. A voice speaking and the listener not yet ready to hear it, to heed its beckoning call in the forest and then a meeting with the speaking tiger. Of necessity, following instructions precisely. The tiger growled but expressed kindness and humility. He listened to the tiger; observed the ripples of its stripes as it spoke. The tiger especially liked the tulip garden and wanted to walk there, all the bright colors of the blooms. Then the next day the tiger woke early: all across the morning sky stretched himself until the brightness of noon negated all trace of animal presence. The hours advanced despite the fact that someone had turned all clocks toward the wall, as if this might slow down or even stall for some moments the onward progression of hours. The moon came up, beckoning the return. Shadows now across the field, two scarecrows and the hum of distant tractors. One shadow aspires, seeks, wants, sees, and so speaks to the scarecrows. They appear not to be actively listening. They watch and wait for the mailman. Sometimes they count backwards: three-two-one. They are impatient; also, immovable. The scarecrows and the shadows lift their faces to the moonlight, take it all into their bodies. The branches of the leafless tree. The roof of the house next door. Part of a telephone pole. Part of a window. Breathing and cancellation. Clean-up. Put away. Check list. Tie shoes. Millions of facts in the night of knowledge. We have a picture of such far away stillness, a bend in the light. At the edge of a stream, something recalled for a moment. Someone starts to speak but only stutters a syllable or two and then stops, looks down at the ground, ashamed. And then a melody: oboe concerto (Bellini). Barely heard but loud enough to lift up, to perk up, to listen, and to find that listening pleasant, worthwhile, and a reason to walk closer to the sound, in its direction which seems to be coming from the nearest town, a small ornamented lyceum built a century before, built when the composer lived, a building built in this small town for just this purpose, for music and its appreciation. One doesn't often think of the oboe, but here, now, it offered many reasons for joy—each note another one. The horses lifted their heads. The sheep and the cows. The swan stayed quiet for once and ceased its honking. Bellini, the opera composer, had written a concerto. All around the fence creatures gathered to listen. When it stopped, the people clapped, the animals bent their heads down to the trough. The walker returned to the creek and recalled the sound, the notes until he could no longer do so. He thought of a kitchen decorated in white tile and black wood. He grew hungry and his stomach growled, but there was nothing to eat. The moon rose and he put his hands in the water.

DAY BY DAY

Those dreamt lines should come back to me. Those are better than the dream of the four-part division. One after another it seems they are in quick succession until morning, that first or second bird's call outside the window where the branches, so lush with green now, appear almost ready to break the glass.

Paul walks with a cane now. There wasn't much I could say when I ran past him this morning for I did not know if the afternoon reception had been planned as a surprise event. Then, too, I didn't want to lie. "How are you?" "Fine, fine." "Why you're looking great!" "Not really." "What do you mean?" Etc. You see. It used to be called Prospect Hill, but they took part of the name out. Taking things out. Yes. I know.

Once more I forgot my opening lines. Oh, well. Wouldn't it have been nice to hear about Rio instead of the humorous anesthesiologist and parti-colored surgical caps? And today the choices are between oils, pastels, or prints. Ice-cream first; followed by an examination of the aesthetic kind. Why do some say "awesome" when clearly what they refer to may be described as ordinary? They have refused to read Burke, or Longinus, *On the Sublime*. I will carry *Paradise* in with me this time convinced, as I am, that Canto XXX holds the key to Stevens's late poem "The River of Rivers in Connecticut." This requires more time.

Psalm 118:24 — This is the day the Lord has made. We will rejoice and be glad in it. This day and all the days before us filled with light and air; filled with ricotta for the cannoli on the table, a round table that occasionally wobbles and that is made out of distressed wood.

They say: when it rains it pours. I say: look out for more (of me). I followed the same path, the same circular route as the day before and as the day before that and tomorrow — yet once again down Fern back on Asylum and et cetera. This repetition is not purgatory; it is — for now, for here — paradise. Remember that this time one year ago we had spent a hot afternoon climbing the stairs up to the top of the Duomo. Quite a view. At some point in time, however, every tourist, every pilgrim and penitent must descend.

A Venetian calm may be just what the dining room requires. Its atmospheric mist and pink tones would add to the tranquility of the nearby blue and green. And a basket encircled by red, a basket holding magazines, cleaned-out once or twice per year. Guests might browse through an issue of *Connecticut Explored* surprised to find that the Alberses lived in a typical suburban raised-ranch tract house. Here they lived their atypical lives.

"Purveyor of life," Sandeep Jauhar has written, "the heart is also its Grim Reaper." An obvious place for some sort of ending, but we must go back up the mountain to the other side where the river flows with water sweet as honey.

After we hang the Venetian scene by Henry Cooke White who also lived on this street, I will say, looks good, and I will look at the image and discover there, two people I know walking by the Doge's Palace, my niece and her husband. How can this be? In New Mexico we saw the people line-up at the sacred site awaiting their chance at a miracle. We saw the spiral staircase that according to engineering science should not stand.

And here in this chair, feet firmly resting upon the floor, I look out the window in the direction of the birdsong and recall the hawk that sat upon the fence a week before and looked as if all traffic would be directed by his wing.

So he said to me, this sort can rarely be genetic and usually can be traced to environmental factors and I said, so that explains it, I grew up in New Jersey. Chuckled then. And how many weeks ago was that conversation?

Take the words from the dictionary and carry them with you in circumstances pleasing or depressing. Remember how Pascal D'Angelo suffered in an ice storm.

One revolves slowly and refers to another realm. It represents the lyrical. The response so burdened becomes impossible. Good-bye to transformation and undeniable markings.

And after there would be a parade, but the new design for the town common had not yet been completed. The hardware store had permanently closed and the building become "available." The bakery opened early. It had expanded into the space next door. The Congregational church displayed the date 1852 in large gold numbers. Up a slight incline a late nineteenth-century Italianate villa had been painted yellow some years ago. It needs repainting, and the cupola blew off in the October storm.

Put either foot forward when ready to begin. Count the days, but not the steps taken in each of those days. The old dirt path will be paved and even the carpenter will find his walkway changed into a driveway. Should the Dutch scenes be saved then we must consider where to hang them. The man near the bridge cannot find his dog and sadness overwhelms him. The doors of the church open slightly and he can hear the singing from inside. His spirits lift for some moments.

Here the river has been contained in pipes buried below ground. The engineer, on occasion, reaches in and moves things around a bit so that they are certain to move along. The engineer contemplates paragraphs in spring, a rise of elevation necessary for the continued maintenance of all required parts. Let's hear what he has to say before we make our judgment, our own estimate of the facts.

Later we might return to the scene with clearer vision, we might move north to south. Gone fishing — the sign left at the door or this one somewhat similar but of no relation, "Wise men fish here." Yes, that location had been well-stocked. Now, long abandoned.

What to sell, what to save, what to store: these are the decisions to be made. And the documents, all of them must be photocopied for the paperless office.

The news has not been inspiring. There are too many parts and each one has been predetermined to fail at some point. The analyst's task is to estimate the time and place of breakdown and prepare each person for the inevitable. The analyst gives one many questions to answer. In this way, each person remains busy and does not become distressed. The program may succeed (even if the person does not).

An advanced model increases the number by one. In so doing, a flame continues to lean in one direction but does not diminish or fade. The crow stands nearby on its green rock and nods with approval all day and all night.

On Sundays we rest. We eat our muffins and drink our coffee. Sometimes the paper arrives before we're up; sometimes we must wait for it. The oldest continuously published newspaper begins to look like the smallest newspaper in America.

He rose and walked round the hall not once as suggested, but three times. This stroll sent him home where he called the objects on the shelves, the images on the walls — talismans. Gladly, he would follow his assigned regimen. If anything, restraint became necessary less he push off toward some distant coast or sprint to the summit of our state's highest place and when atop sing non-stop sacred spirituals Gospel hymns of unending joy.

To record the thoughts of idle reverie — and worry. To move out of the past and into the present and on to the future. The fiercest agonies have the shortest reign. Those are the words of the poet who in Turin attended a church service such as could not be shared on Long Island.

But these matters offer only momentary disguise for the real matter at hand. Should the laying-on of hands be tried? In New Mexico miracles worked each morning. In the dusty yard before the sanctuary were cast off crutches, abandoned braces, and even one glass eye thought at first to be a child's lost marble.

Wait for tomorrow. You will go to sleep and then it'll seem you merely blinked your eyes and you'll wake up and it'll be over. First, two feet will wiggle once again and then animation will work its way up from there. In the mind, a mountain may be climbed; a race, run. In the mind, a government might cancel your permit; refuse to allow your expedition. Back in the city square, chess players will take their contest seriously, remain oblivious to musicians as moves and countermoves play out. How much might bystanders gamble on one player or another? How long must they wait for the results?

Our view out the window looks north. We see a reflection in the window of people walking past, an almost constant stream of them. Everyone very busy. There are options, different ways to get from here to home. Those with blue gloves do not direct traffic. The canopy does not keep out all the rain. Quiet now — awaiting their beef broth or carrots and meat loaf. A word or two and then a pause. Even a ballpoint pen feels heavy. Dim the lights to protect the eyes. Things keep rolling. Here comes the Jell-O cart. In China two Canadian citizens have been detained. Blue wrap around tall buildings. Some wear a blue belt as they walk down the hall to return today's newspaper to the lounge. Look at the headlines. Someone got it. They ate everything. Nothing remains.

I have been crucified with Christ. My arms pulled back and flesh severed and the bones broken. My feet swollen and lungs filled with fluid. My groin severed and my abdomen sliced. Always a level of pain controlled and tolerable because absorbed by those who came before me. And what will be our task?

Our professor told us for the final project in his class to look to the future. What does that mean, we asked? He said, I'm not sure. And after a pause: but try it. And so we did, but as we were doing so and making notes on our predictions and visions our pens ran out of ink. Now what do we do, we wondered? And our semester had ended, our professor had left for Italy. One of us said that it didn't really matter. We had seen the future and did not care for it. Now hold on a second, another member of our class interrupted. I like what I saw very much, thank you. The future will be wonderful. What I want to do, the classmate continued, is to tell others what we have seen, the marvels to come. And a third doubted the efficacy of such prophecy. This member asserted, no one will believe you. The people have eyes but do not see. The people have ears but will not listen to you. The people have tongues with which they will hurl darts of slander at you. You should sit on the balcony, they said.

And then the sun came out. People crossed the street, they moved along to wherever they meant to go. A man in a uniform took off his hat, and he held it in his hands close to his heart. A man with an umbrella used it to steady himself as he crossed the street, slowly, to the other side.

The park from the western loop to the eastern overlook (believe in something — science, Moses — something). Tennis courts, baseball fields, a gray heron in the pond, dahlias, Ana Grace Marquez-Greene Playground (the Spirit blows where it will). And then home again via the woodchip trail. The tallest redwood in Connecticut. The oldest house on the block (1845) later expanded and absorbed in that expansion (1873). Tiger lilies in bloom along the drive. "When people come together in reconciliation and forgiveness, one can be sure it is the work of the Divine spirit." That's what Father Joe said.

What's it all for? Here I am standing around freezing
In this over air-conditioned room, a black band on my arm
While you lie now so still, slumber, even, hardly breathing.

I, too, saw a light that came and that's now receding
Into some dark station, some zone far beyond an old barn.

What's it for? Here I am twiddling my thumbs, freezing.
"Christ Died For Our Sins": white letters fading against a red wall;
A structure leans each ephemeral year closer to the hay-brown lawn
While you lie now so still, slumber even, hardly breathing.

Who was it that painted such over-sized, bold lettering,
Visible from every tidy corner of this suburbanized farm?
"Christ Died For Our Sins." What's it all for anyway?
I stand around dumb, freezing. All these houses, boxes really,
Built to hide all this dying. A nameless soul painted those

Words, a borrowed charm maybe. And now you lie so still,
Slumber even: breathing? There are no horses, no fields, and
No flowers, not anymore. Those old red structures are,
Usher-like, pointless, incessantly tossed into the tarn.

What's it all for? Here I am standing around freezing
While you lie now so still, slumber even, hardly breathing.

He goes down to the pool and paints children and their parents; he
paints floats in the shape of turtles and television monsters; he paints
the bright colors of an inflatable beach ball. Back upstairs we try a trop-
ical iced tea and he recalls early years in Maine. He asks us about the
Whites, who for some time lived in the large Queen Anne style house
up the block before moving to Waterford. We tell him we used to live
in the carriage house there and how cozy we found it. He asks who lived
in the main house at that time. And we say an orthodontist and his
family. He seems somehow saddened by the fact. Oh, yes, he says. I can
see a connection, a heritage. Work done by hand with tools and what
difference brushes or drills. But we understand. Three generations of

painters, a calling forth of the beautiful versus something much more practical: the call of career, job, money, income, and material doodads. He asks us, and what of the spirit? Is the point something more than food and shelter? We say we have not a clue and think that from his present perspective he might better inform us.

Nothing extraordinary, just the usual basic metabolic and CBC panel. I'll have to be driven and then when I get there, hope that a usable vein can be found and stuck without too much discomfort. I may return to my normal lifestyle with moderation in three weeks. Continue taking these medications ... One wonders why the vein on the left-hand has become slightly enlarged and sensitive to the slightest pressure. One wonders if there might be any connection between a tumor on a heart-valve and a tumor on a kidney (lower pole right-side). One wonders how a kidney functions if it has been reduced and sutured. One wonders, what exactly does the surgeon do during a robotic procedure? (The east coast is like a pinball machine.)

This month. This scene. These slices of peach. These sounds. And the aroma of lilac, the hotel patio that explains it. Count the days before, the days after. This paragraph. This vision. These decisions. And each one has been predetermined, the travel difficult. Give in one direction, you see the price. This drive in the car. This turn. These years. These physicians. And another one from Primrose Hill, the images on the walls. Say I can, the tranquility of blue. This tourist. This day and every day. These shirts. These familiar sounds. And in the drawer of a desk, the sign. Gone fishing, gone to see. This I picked up and this I moved. These doors. These old barns. And I suppose on occasion an outline offered. Take the machine, the show. This yesterday and those trees, those flowers; orange ones in a red pot and yellow ones in a blue one. Give instructions, the frame. This view out the window. This longest day. Those temperatures that rise. Those highways. And this balm, the reward gained. See the parade, the matinee. This production. This jitterbug. Those sixteen miles. And these remains. And

I don't recall having fallen asleep, the afternoon. Start the music, we will drive. This bright sunlight. This better.

You go to sleep and in a blink wake-up and it'll all be over. In the east the sun rises. Sitting on a bench its rays strike you, and you try to remember. Was I awake, you ask? Recall wheels of the cart turning on the hard surface and someone saying here's a small bump and then the elevator to a room that overlooked both the original building (the oldest building) and the newest one, though there wasn't much opportunity to stand by the window and look around. What you did see appeared bowl-like, edges of green that sloped down to a contained urban space crisscrossed by streets.

On the bench, Sunday paper in hand, sunlight warms my face. It doesn't matter what's in the news or what stories the body's skin reveals. These rays and their warmth feel good; yes, they brighten up this day. I can smell coffee (not roses). I will shower. I will walk, read, and write. I will live. I will rise again tomorrow: sun up over the Travelers Tower (1906, Donn Barber). I like this building and this day and all the days to follow. I will run again and see other buildings, too, those celestial towers also tapered but unimaginable.

Focus on what is real, not what you imagine (the fracture of self-help).

> remove *m* from them and
> get the
> (don't move,
>   don't breathe)
> breath
> collection of phrases and
> successive positions of I
> sun wheel night to
> understand

become rain or mist
become white of white sheets
passion always
to behold its object
needs a perfect unit
bringing this
into equilibrium
with the world
be its I engaged

In the waiting room I read a book called *A Death of One's Own*. It said that most of all the spouse must not forget. I jotted some notes then about the Verrazano Bridge but soon realized I had forgotten what body of water it goes across. I chuckled a little bit and then it was my turn to enter.

And John Adams had claimed of this day, "the most memorable," but no one remembers and dates get confused, an erroneous one credited for the birth of this nation. And within the body politic an illness spreads that no surgery can resection and then suture with success for tomorrow and all the days to follow in a grand Republic.

And yet the follow-up to come may be assuring, the growth snipped, no need for alarm, no fear of Apocalypse, stay on the path, stick to the prescribed plan, be sure to do your part, and you'll see mountain laurel like never before. Eyes alert to the blossom and the branch, you'll take a hike in the light of an orange sun. These lessons your old friend offers and these you have learned. When a gathering takes place along a ridgeline, you'll say remember and he'll say predict. Okay, you'll agree, if we start from here we will go forward. The only direction the knees bend, he'll joke but then you'll add, that's an old story. Let's see how this new one progresses. We can walk. We'll get there and when we reach that fence we can climb over or we can find a gate, open it, and then pass through it to the next mown field.

FORTUNES

Tell the truth about the bloodworm's chances to survive. Tell the horse all about its clumsy dance partner who lives very happily inside an enlarged intestine and the copperhead who slithers on the floor frightening old horses to the very end of their tether, to the very rear of their cage. Tell the poor creatures not to worry about who it is that crawls about in the dark cavern to avoid a fisherman's rusted hook, a trout's sharp teeth, while the poor host kicks at the dirt and repeats its last meal. Tell the cautious fisherman the story about the one who ran into the lake chased by a snake that rolled over the water like a magic wheel from one side to the other. Tell the truth about hoop snakes and copperheads to all the children who need to be warned and to all the fishermen who don't believe in magic, to all the wives alone now that the snake has come. Tell me how to fend for myself in the dark, how to stay out of the lake, out of the horse's midsection. Who has the talisman that can protect the innocent? Who has the wafer that can redeem the fallen? Tell the truth about the bloodworm's chances. Tell the truth about mine. I can take it.

from Frame Narrative

THE HOUSE STYLE

That's the house style

Flipping through, I could see how
much I didn't remember

He would chuck, he would,
as much as he could

What happened to Isaac?

That's the house style

They like a bit of romance
but not so much

It's hard to call someone a friend

That's the house style

He would chuck, he would

Washington *fiore fiume fuori*
A cousin in Oslo?

Not us O Lord
Not us

Flower, river—the house style

Outside he would

And did

BAEDEKER

To the north, a bare hill
The sky a mixture of music, food
Vast forests—the beauty not revealing
It was there in every corner

And it will continue in our room
Something good about the paint; our chance, bright
Only in part correct and followed by
Their dark eyes, skin the color of bronze

This is what you do then
Serve up the double portion as we gather
This is what you do then
Three levels of high end luxury, the possible

The house was near, dwarfed by distance
Bound up passions, feuds, the palm
Here lay the meaning, they stayed away
Flies swarmed at the table

Here and there was a house drawing light
White in the sun the walls of bare clay
Narrow barred windows fierce and embarrassed
Other quarters as if bow legs and blank eyes

Gave an effect shapeless and wrinkled
Out of bounds, impersonal, little breathing-space
Everyone knows the hostile workings of the expense
Half-sunk in the ground and continued

Once upon a time the houses were all alike

Every now and then the doors of some
Never failed to hold the same thing
The paper shiny with a promise

Even to speak to their hearts
Is something constantly never (set)
How to talk what is opposed to stars
The great news never came back

Huddled together with shirt-sleeves rolled
Gray weather and windy, a gentle drizzle
All the players looked out the window
The cards that evening fell

Rough weather turning cold at night
The house in a shapeless ocean
And a wind released from across
The clearing embittered and poor

Snow perhaps the eclipse swung
Between these shadows these precise terms
No appeal for an old palette shapeless
Masses of color elusive, mysterious

In the house a face appeared at the window
This is what you do then
This is what you do then

ALICE

Travel dislodges her from the city.
In a house, another young struggle
For a country, a better life.
Into a house, this great economic
Wealth: in rural communities
Newcomers liked to talk with Alice,
Fretted over woodland, cars. She
Asked them to be assertive, to
Be self-reliant; in a few weeks,

Mobile. In a world where a wife's
Artistic interests did not bruise
Long periods of time, it is not
Hard to see the complexity of
Experience, this mathematical
Satisfaction, tense and anxious.
Ambushed, worried, beginning to
Have pains—the usual picture;
The old, stable church, the anger

Of other women. A rough, competitive
World, the day's battle, traditions:
These mobile parents have not deliberately
Tormented Alice's weekend. They felt
She had her keys in the ignition
Lock. Her children's self-confidence and
Muscle often start on the road. In
Trouble, others join new clubs, keen
To keep up. Alice was beginning to

Depend on strong-minded neighbors.

They were all patient, producing
Anything for the trapped. Builders
Everywhere! Alice in the mornings
Walked out to take the wheel
Feeling of success, building the beginnings
Of recognition. She was powerfully
Multiple in the boom-and-bust. She
Aroused her new home. In a local

Restaurant, something she said,
Something she had begun to think
Waned and companionship troubled her
No longer. Machines handled error,
This fear of a neighbor's waiting at
Home. There is another difference:
Alice got them grape juice and some
Little League teams and Cub Scout
Dens. And then Alice moved to this

World of travail and strife, this
Average parkway character. The
Prosperous people had granite curbs
And sidewalks, woods lined a large
Open field. Sometimes everything
Came to bricks and debris. Alice
Answered her friend, but at the front
Door a blond mother of two children
Prevented the normal turnover seen

Coast-to-coast. It's ridiculous! And
The doors were open to all on Sunday
Mornings. It was apparent that
An extremely important conference

With the cast would have issued
Brochures for political rallies across
Town. Disappointed, Alice produced
Six alternatives. She was told not to go
Back. One woman expected a moment's

Prevention: the exchanges were never
Judged. A small section of homes
Found a resident to adopt, to plan,
To turn carefully. If all the people
Were asked for another sponsored
Night, their status might put a burden
On relations more vitriolic than
One of the scars in this community.
Lead the way, many urged. But Alice

Shrugged off the coffee and wrote
A four-page letter to show respect for
Other members. Hidden money added
An episode that forced everyone
Present to find an idea in their private
Struggles. The highest percentage, some
Thought, mix well in the house next-door.

REPORT A PROBLEM WITH THIS POEM

Mitch Wayne behind a window.
Lucy Moore's legs below an ad in the office.
Lucy's red lips as red as the seat of the cab.
Kyle Hadley and Lucy wear the same color
Business suits. Mitch wears brown:
Brown of the bar; brown of the plane.
In Lucy's hotel room: Mitch in a mirror
Between Kyle and Lucy. Lucy has a soda
At the drugstore. Mary Lee Hadley drinks
In a bar. Mary Lee and Mitch at a party:
Two half-empty glasses in the foreground.
Drugs. Drugs. Drugs. And a little boy
On a rocking horse. At another restaurant,
Lucy sits between Mitch and Kyle. Jasper
· Hadley and Mitch look out a window
At Mary Lee being brought home.
Mary Lee dances with Mitch's photograph.
Jasper has a heart attack.
Lucy and her red lips again, now in a red
Seat in the library. Mitch still in brown.
Mary Lee and Kyle framed in a window
Looking out at Lucy and Mitch.
Brick wall. Kyle's face. All eyes on Kyle.
No idyll. Suggestion of blackmail.
Mitch says, "How far we've come . . . "
Mitch and Lucy ride off: last image, a gate.

FLICKED BY FEELING

Something transfixed and transfixing
In such jazzed-up gibberish as
To offer hymns instead of hotels

Something sensed as being so senseless—
A demise taken, not given, and therefore
An end without a beginning but for those

Stanzas stretched and then delivered
Such tokens cannot purchase freedom
From the most bemused bewilderment

What holds still can only be a question
Unanswered even if often asked—
This suburban sublime frightful and dark

PAST PERFECT

The fact was we needed money.
There were the expenses and then
There were the loans. Word of mouth
Led me to the job: I taught and
I shared an office, a windowless

Concrete office, filled floor to ceiling
With directories. I carried a briefcase
Purchased in London. It contained
A sort of flesh-colored leather
On the inside. The store had been

Full of umbrellas. A briefcase seems
An affectation, but I would not
Leave it behind. It might be
In a closet. It might have a handle
And two bright gold locks beside.

REPENTANCE

I never lock my door.
I don't know if the lock works.

I had dozed off one day while
Reading; then startled awake

By shuffling sounds in the narrow
Though high-ceilinged room. When

I opened my eyes to the bright
Light of the sun setting over the mountains

In the west, the presence of Wallace
In the room surprised me. We

Are not friends. And there he stood
Amid the few feet possible to stand

In the narrow space. I said hello
And he told a brief joke, bowed slightly,

And left. I rolled over, grabbed my pillow,
But could not sleep again, and so got up.

I looked out the window. It would
Be a pleasant evening. But

When I looked on the dresser my five
Dollars was gone, money I'd need later

That night. It had to have been there,

Sent earlier in the week from New Jersey

By my mother. And now it was gone.
Wallace had absconded with it: my

Thursday night beer money! He reappeared
At my door. Brazenly. He told me

To ask him if he had a match. I played
Along. "Do you have a match?" I asked.

He replied, "Not since Shakespeare died."
He turned and walked down the hall.

Strange, I thought, and then I thought:
The perpetrator returns to the scene of the crime.

Had he attempted to throw me off the chase?
Later that night I went to the pub

Even though, without pub-funds.
I would say it is my birthday.

That would make up for the sudden
And unexpected loss of funds. Wallace

Sat at the bar, hamburger in hand,
Purchased with my money. I

Did not want violence and so sought
Diplomacy. I greeted Wallace and

Asked, "Do you have match?"

He replied, "Not since Shakespeare died."

He then tapped the barstool next to him
Thus, inviting me to take a seat. I did

And soon the conversation switched to Nietzsche.
Wallace offered to buy me a beer in honor of my birth.

UNPACK IT

Once more I have come to Hartford as
A ship moves into light and open space.

At the edge of language, frustrated and
Tired, yet at the same time, arrived!

(Hard on the page; then torn limb by limb,
Like so many words through a vice.)

Here smoke disappears, not the long solo
Nor the final bow, or the beat of any two hearts.

Resolved: small shadow of footsteps, mere
Accident of local circumstance, and

A certain lightness of our former days—
Do not immerse this or use it with a control device.

Return once more to the window, and
See the brown-winged bird attempt flight.

Existence is a remembered and repeated thing.

ALTERNATING CURRENT (*Excerpt*)

You walk by the University, the old building.
It is a new district for you since you have not
Walked here before. It is so quiet at this hour,
Cold and quiet. Along the back of the

Antiquities museum there is a large open
Garden with benches along its side.
At the other end of it and across a narrow
Street an even narrower drive leads to

The courtyard of one of the few official
Dormitories. No one stirs at this hour
Of the day. You think, there is no other
Like it. Enough is enough, though, you

Decide, and retrace your steps to the genteel
Neighborhood in which you live. Along
The way, you pass the narrowest of houses,
The morning's first tour boat—near

Empty—sliding beneath a bridge, a fishmonger
Rolling back the boards that cover his stall
Each night. This is where you live and although
You do not know any of the people you pass,

You nod to some and say hello to some, good
Morning to others. Then a tram bell rings
And the world brightens.

from sound / hammer

MEMOIR

The knees are the eyes of the legs.
By them I am never transfixed,

but rather transported to where
I want to go. They will never

return me to where I have been:
amorphous or amphibian.

At each turning point they have
never failed to turn: first from

cell to soul and then to something
I have yet to understand. My

knees seem to know what's
next, even in the dark.

NIGHT WALK

Our boots were by the door. We were ready to enter
the cold as soon as we opened the door and stepped

outside. How surprised we were when we did so and
felt the mild night air. We turned left and noted

the right side lights had been turned off, possibly
removed, but the left side ones glowed. We turned

left and proceeded straight, uneventfully, though
we had hoped to see an animal. When we made our

next left hand turn, we saw lights approaching us.
At the last moment, they veered off to our left, their

right. Soon, they disappeared. We heard voices,
but couldn't place them nor could we locate their

source. Then we saw an animal, a little farther ahead,
enough so that we could not distinguish its chief

characteristics and hence: its species. So silent:
we noted as we turned left once more. We stepped

inside and placed our boots neatly by the door,
hats and gloves beside.

BLACKOUT

From a joyless beach
small craft give safe

passage, the cursing made
plain by rule.

In its talking—
what does it say?

Without cards, a keel scrapes
into sedge, stops and

goes with the body
elongated by delay.

In its talking—
what does it say?

The strangeness of it:
such turbid air and one's wish

to know mirrors,
skin and bone.

FORENSIC

We found him
in a pool of words.

They might have been his
but that is uncertain.

THE BALCONY

Don't be so naïve, Dennis.
Here, let me give you one example.

My mother lives alone in a small
apartment on the edge of Naples.

My father died when we were young.
She lives several floors up and it is

difficult for my mother to manage
the stairs. She wanted a balcony—

to get some air and sun. She
doesn't have much and this is all

she wanted, a balcony. A contractor
came and quoted a price and

they agreed. Work began. The
workers drilled into the wall of my

mother's small apartment on the edge
of Naples. Then they left and did not

return. The contractor came. He said:
there must be a payment before we continue,

before we conclude. She said, no,
a price has been agreed upon,

a price has been paid, and he

said, they will break my workers' legs

if we proceed. I do not wish
this, he said, neither the violence

nor the payment. There were those holes
and, besides, she still wanted the balcony.

That was all she wanted. She paid.
What was she to do: one elderly

woman in a small apartment on the
edge of Naples?

ARS POETICA

In my head I hear Marcello
in the midst of *la dolce vita*.

In my head I picture Marcello
in an empty piazza—*piazza
vuota*—a fountain overflowing
with angst and Marcello,
cigarette in hand, staring pensive
but nowhere in particular, watching
some birds in the near distance,
wondering perhaps when a few
friends will return, slowly smoking
that cigarette.

Though I have never
smoked, I understand the semiotic
utility: a man and a woman go
out somewhere, sometime—probably
late, later than I would ever consider
going out (I must stay at home
so that I may write this).

The man
and the woman say nothing, but they
have their cigarettes to occupy them,
to close the canyon between them.
They stare and inhale and exhale
and say nothing.

Now everything
has changed.

They must speak but this
guarantees nothing.
Before there may have been
something to do, but now they are so
desperate for something to do because
they still have nothing to say.

Oh, Marcello, Marcello: here
is an opportunity for the poet.

PASTURE

Am I now a farmer? Frail, but not
fragile; slow, yet not immobile, I

decide what the scythe cuts.
Mornings are for reading. My

kingdom requires odes and eclogues.
The old songs I used to sing

recalled now by ghost or skeleton are
spirits through which another scythe

must pass. Significant events begin
in exact origins, gray and black,

here a breath, but less than sound—
visible notions of permission—the stone

later. Results show the punch line:
candlelight and music, a picture

divided then carried across the shoulder.

ALBUM

Red leaves out from their leather binding.
Red leaves that had been pictures for us.
Once they were in your home, in my home.
Red leaves glued to the album of forgetfulness.
Red leaves from our travels west, to the beach.
Red leaves that we pointed to
and then cried, "Look."
Red leaves pulled from the past
and burned in the fire.
Red leaves between us.
Red leaves from the first weekend and the last.
Red everywhere and nowhere:
lost in syllables of regret.

LAMENTATIONS

It is the gap I fell into
yet neither a new planet
nor a black hole. I might
have been alone even
if others were present.
And what could I have
said to them or told
myself? I noted the wall-
paper and its coincidence.
We were gathered in our
hometown yet everything
felt so foreign.

Outside the younger kids
rode their bikes north
to the park or south into
town. On Main Street
someone parked their car
in the pharmacy lot to pick
up a prescription and
someone else pulled along
the curbside by Pietro's to
pick up a pizza to bring
home for dinner. Some hike
in the near-distant hills
and others stumble from
the Trackside Inn.
The six o'clock train arrives
and then departs for the next
town. Everything spins
except inside where we wait

still as stone for tall ships
and fireworks, for celebrations
of all sorts planned by
committees handpicked.

I am too much who I am
and not enough anyone else.
What if we confess?
There were years before
we met and plenty of time
apart even after we met
in heavy wind and rain.
It has been six months
already! And if I confess?
Never did my spirits
require to be tranquilized
by quiet and repose.
I could go six miles or
so with my head held in
my hands. I would, too.
I might be the only one
honest enough to confess.
I am who I am.
Just ask.

A child becomes sick and the
doctor is summoned, but the
child dies. And the doctor
arrives on a donkey and the
child's father throws the
donkey off a cliff. The
father moves to America.
His son buys a motorcycle.

The father sees it inside the
house and the father throws
it down the stairs.

Arise, woman and weep in the night.
At the dawn of your vigil open your
heart wide as the oceans. In praise
of God raise up your hands
for the breath of children weak now
with hunger at the end of each street

Hoard of Jerusalem:
hunger in Hebrew is *raav*,
a snake in an empty mouth.

    After Erri De Luca

THE LIBRARY (*After Paul Eluard*)

Absent my cola day here
absent my puppet at the harbor
absent the table absent the edge

absent the image *soirée*
absent the arms career
absent a corona day's riot

absent the marvel the tweet
absent the pain block the journal
absent the season's finances

absent too my shift on aware
absent the tank so late and noisy
absent the black loon I so wanted

absent the stamps' lure eyes on it
absent the aisles may also
absent the million days *hombres*

absent the mouse my new age
absent the sewers the courage
absent a blue epaulet faded

absent the forms skin still wants
absent the coaches' gay colors
absent a tan physique

absent the sentences evil says
absent the routes deployed
absent the places key to boredom

absent my mansion reunited
absent fruit copied in dough
absent my minor Etna chamber

absent my sheen go man it tundra
absent sense orioles addressed
absent melancholy melody, night

absent the trembling demand for day
absent the odd jets of mint air
absent the photo few bit

absent a *touché* accordion
absent the front of my animus
absent shock its tent key

absent the victory day surprises
absent the levers a tent gives
absent an Odysseus to silence

absent my refuge the truth
absent the fairest and cruelest days
absent the mirth the moon and

absent what solitude knows
absent the marches to the morgue
absent the sanity we renewed

absent the risk that too
absent missed parts absent sylvan air

and for the favor done
you recommence my feet

LILAC

You need to remember
that it was snowing
little words that backfired.
Then you need to remember that
labor is nothing fancy,
nothing at all more than
or less than wing beats
of geese off in the distance.
All the colors of Mondrian's

Boogie-woogie collapse, ever-
darkening our chamber. Now
closer to bloom, I recall
shampoo and leather. The
taste of turkey on my tongue
offers up rough occasion;
some texture to a world
far from those distant geese
and their incessant honking.

Reunion within the triangle:
forty citizens of Paris may exit
the frame; others may enter.
Off to one side a line forms our
boundary of sight. If I could
make myself the *gendarme* of this
scene my arm would rise
as if to mimic the structure's
steel, halt these walkers moving

into and then out of the frame.
Halt—my signal would say

and then I would add "look"
and continue "we are in a
city of lights" and *voilà* the tower
would glow as forty or so
citizens of Paris pause to remember
where they are and I would say
"ça va" and I would say

"*maintenant*" and a split second
later I would know that I had
decided my figure in the center,
the one with the *chapeau*, that was me
turning another image sideways
to see the length of those lines and
across town our mayor counts
potted blooms hoping for tourists
far beyond all accumulated harvest.

Our neighbors have prepared the flowers,
the fruit, and the cloth. I stand as we
proceed down the boulevard and
my little brother looks up to me.
I do not fall as we proceed, as we
march on and on. I find courage
enough to look into our kitchen.
The lights come on as I enter and
once more I hear Ozzie and Harriet

argue about dinner as if it will be
their last meal. Such pilgrims hesitate.
They wonder what will be. They turn
sideways to predict the length of their
lives and their footsteps move beyond those French
doors and jangle through a sharp-edged book.

ANIMAL RESCUE

I am on a park bench
sitting with legs crossed and
hands folded, looking toward
dogs way off beyond the pond.

I wait and think about those dogs
running across that hill while I sit
granite-like on the bench made of
wood, a pebble of sorts, lost.

What we remember may be our
home of first address even at the last.
You call out and I turn but
when I look you aren't there.

from Parallel Lines

WHAT LASTS

There is a reason for all the ripples
and the still protests beyond.
There is a reason for vacancies in the sky;
a reason for dark objects
that mark and configure a shore.

The reason is this:
one frayed rope of light
binds persistent space and ties
the ocher curl of a final cockspur
leaf to that rippled surface.

LIVING ROOM

The word *family* has come to mean
Fewer and fewer people

I myself am the emblem of the form

Rhyme, a word to end the line
But not the sentence

The blue of the eyes
Is not the blue of the sea

Why is the child a gleam
In the father's eyes

Fit a mold and be
Remodeled

PARENTING

We chose not to
It wasn't an easy decision
Often I daydream
But never incessantly
I want to be precise
This doesn't keep me
Awake at night
And yet
Can you imagine?

DOCUDRAMA

A window repairman came to repair
a window where a bird had flown
into it and broke it. The next day another
bird met its match on the window's mate.

Poetry is the absence of insurance.

In another room another man spoke about a woman
in a language that could not be understood and he
kept close count of his pulse as he struck the ivory
keys on an out-of-tune piano and remembered.

Poetry is the absence of insurance.

SCARF (*Excerpt*)

This camera is not alert.
a clause is a sentence
a clause in a memorable sentence
a sentence in a short story
a sentence in a story by a
forgotten writer
a clause in a sentence a story
memorable but unread
unread because the writer has been
forgotten, obscured
remember how he worked
for his own obscurity
and that of others
he devoted his life to his own
obscurity and that of others
some of the others on occasion
may be recalled thanks
to his efforts while he
is not

In the dawn he wakes
His camera is not alert
A man stands by
an open window
Does he yawn or does he sing?

"John, come here. Look at my feet."
"What is it, dear?"
"See that toe?"
"Which one?"
"The third one. See it?"

"Which foot?"

"The right one."

"What is it?"

"You see it?"

"Yes."

"Well?"

"What is it? What am I supposed to see?"

"That toe."

"What about it?"

"That toe. It is not mine."

"What?"

"That toe is not my toe."

"Well, whose is it?"

"I don't know. I just noticed it—that it's not mine, I mean."

"It looks like yours."

"No. No, mine was different."

"In what way, dear?"

"In every way, John."

"How do you know?"

"Just look at it, John. Just look at it. It isn't me. It isn't mine."

"Are you sure? I don't . . ."

"Yes, I'm sure."

"Well, then. There's only one thing to do."

"I know. I thought so, I mean."

"We'll have to remove it. You'll have to lose the toe before we lose all of you."

"I'm ready now. Go and get your saw. I will still be here when you return."

At my present age
he was already seven
years dead.

"If I had a dog, John, I'd
name her Spout. 'Down,
Spout. Down, Spout'."

Perhaps we should think in terms
of opera?

The sports star's fall from grace
    or the politician's rise to power?

What seems to be the problem, Officer?

Bones are / the die is

Something small holds on to a leg,
cheek pressed tight to that leg.

And then is dragged . . .

MAP

A song of bridges
And then a silence

At one time
There were no stones

Oak rippled water
And an oar-less boat

At night: darkness
As expected; then morning

A wing that beats
The silence back

PERFECT SIX

History is the end of all things eternal.
The a-historical bee never exits the hive.
We remember Achilles. Then recall that
He died. Sometimes we can glimpse
The pacing, the placing of our returns from
The theoretical to the autobiographical.
A door may open: the thing to do is enter.

LEGACY

Efficiency is the death of poetry.
A foundation survives to
Reveal such small dimension.
Our skeletons grow
Weary and other voices start
Singing X Y Z,
X Y Z. Memory remains
Intimate. The clock strikes:
Cakes we called "the fingers
Of the Holy Apostles." We lived
Closed fisted and greedy of filthy
Lucre: efficient. And I
Hesitate to say this but
(and repeat over and over again

HERE ARE THE STONES

Where are the workers?
Stones remain.
A line of hammers struck
but the workers left
for the suburbs.
Here are the stones.
Where are the workers?
The owner paid well
—carver and quarryman—
took care of them
when they got sick. God bless
him. Here
are the stones. Where
are the workers?
Stones cut workers inside
out. Workers cut stones
outside in. Trees reclaim
yards and beds. The dead
below rest without
memorial or marker, far
from any suburb elysian.
But the owner lives on:
in town, school, street, store,
and more. Our guide says:
he was a kind God.

THE BIG PUSH

The radius never expanded
And the planet always
Circled the sun, but at

Age twenty-four, one
Doesn't feel it turning.
Then—all of a sudden—

At age sixty, one stands
Still and senses that larger
Movement; thinks then

There are no answers.
The fact of an address does
Not solve the situation.

Names change. Memory
Finds a place to live
In the barren gray woods

Of December. My tent has
Been pitched. I'll row
A canoe down the river

Just so I can recall its name.
Some say the neighbors are
Unfriendly, more reticent

Than any Mayflower descendant.
Let silence enlarge and keep us
All as clean as snow.

from The Walls of Circumstance

RECRUIT

Mix all items carefully, but only mash what you have first secured with string. Beat down the blossoms before the hoary wind lifts them up and away. Raise your own flag instead of theirs and call yours "belabored one." Stroke it. Be sure to cover all the bases prior to any exchange of allegiances. Gather any sacred tablets mandatory for a post-operative performance and swallow. Force grandfather time into some very tight corners and twist, or face the cruel punch delivered by the harshest disciplinarian. Roll with it, but never before you cover it. Just to be safe, gild the coterie. Slide your left hand along our patron's backside and press hard on the most embarrassing spaces. Keep pressing until something pleasant occurs. Then dip below to remove the excess.

METRONOME

A jet fighter's fuselage imitates Icarus and his waxen wings too far from where it started the day, too late for rescue. The pilot dies; a village simmers. The reporter's voice stirs, then blazes—briefly, then sticks inside the throat and turns to ash. Some want the lyre and the dance and coziest trysts. Some learn that the guise means fanatic. Get up; stop the sour ode and its swarthy reflections. We've all been vanquished by the bomb and by those lively apparitions. After the clanging that lifts my ego from this sordid tomb, the sky is clear again of belabored fists. A solo dancer crosses the forest. His song hangs there, an existence that outlasts syllables, yet never sells. What dark wisdom between floorboards and windows rises with sleep? All our mirrors are tautologies. Disinter those bones from their frame and pocket them in your dream. Reduce them, if they haven't been already, to an ashen, unnerved shade that clings to the shivering arms of a burnished oak. Take precautions. Prior to flight fold your tent into the figure of a carousel. Commemoration does not take flight, but roots in a faith turned fallow by doubt. Now our armies have their arrows pointed home; Achilles has his brown shoes buffed and clean. He'll be wearing the black gloves and leading the parade in four-four time. He's been lying low. Divine prophecy spins upward while human happiness handholds accounts so tight (eyes closed and arms crossed) that their numbers as on wires pass through the epidermis charged and ever changing. Some say that no animals kill their own offspring, yet I have seen the crows outside pick tiny bird-bones religiously. Some say that the younger you are the more innocent you are, free from the flame that singes the middle-aged. Some say that the flame is red and others call it crimson, but no one knows the name of the man who wears it.

THE FIRST LINE OF DEFENSE

In my heart is the house. In the painting hang all roads. Funerals, I suppose. A dark, disconcerting friend had dreams the sap awoke. Alone in a house he passes a table, a whole charm in its way. At a temple you finally think you've met the master and I mix a mess of toads each day and for years I wrote poetry. Leave the garden. The master has felt his brains, a kiss like the glorious war in the alpine. How can I thank you, the voice I demand? If I have existed, I have seen a few words. I sit down in our village. The back of the closet hangs in a kind of prison, a volcano flashing in the night. She has been a long day, delight: forest fire. It was raining. Lately, I've been drifting. The technology in traffic signals changes almost continually, the weather. Her visits with oil were lovely that year. When he was opening his play in the house, in the ruins of my youth, she kissed me. I was eighteen then. We have afternoon and the university—the mad contralto at the door. An old man becomes an erasure, becomes a friend's dying. Every day I close my eyes, remember just the cold. The technology in traffic signals changes almost continually.

THE MAY SWEEPS

I was hoping to hang a hammer from my hip. The white sofa needed new upholstery so that the sea of blue-green wall-to-wall would not clash with the orange slices we chewed so mercilessly or the television test pattern that flickered so softly, so candle-like over in the corner. We would sit side by side on this sofa and put fences between us, another reason for the hammer. But years later others came along and painted the hospital white walls a baby's blanket blue. They took the carpet away, tied up all those dear memories in little rolls and left them at the curb. True, a sofa still sat there in the same spot as before, but the fences were gone even though the address remained the same. And for a while the new owners watched all that wheeled their bouncing ball along. They watched without worry, without shame, without loss, envy, or anger. Now they, too, are gone. They ascended a ladder that took them far away from here.

PICKPOCKETS

They use tools, sliding whistles, and long, slender hands to take readers to the place they want them to go. Then they start to sing about the simplest things, the unnoticed things: the gum wrapper at our feet, the air outside this room, the geometric patterns of telephone wires and poles. They think they know it all and tell us so and try to entwine us into their lives. They try to remake us, to get us to vote some other way, to give up umbrellas in the rain or to use more sunscreen at the beach. And then there's all that talk about meaning and involvement, vision and music. They have their definitions, their transformations and self-regulations; their complexes into which they'd have us enter. They are noxious with their self-regulating rhythms and their symmetries and repetitions. They might have been the greatest help to us if not for the fact that general algebra failed to set them straight, failed to pull them back from their palettes and parallel scenes. They will attempt to integrate us behind the black ink of their phrases or by elaborating on letters previously sent. What is it to be real? They ask as one of us falls and another draws hot soup lipward. Indeed, says another, just try it! They decline, retreat, and hide, leaving room for a box of actual chocolates, for a rose set in a glass on the table.

WILLOW-TWIGS

A land of leaning ice burst above the coconut palms of these porous hands. Be with me, I cried, oh, brazen hypnotic. Forgetfulness is like a popular song, short and sweet. Words came to me one night, green rustlings greeting the dawn and its woven rose-vines. Here my chill enters from the sea: tall, nameless, and late at night. This dinosaur of evening is an island of infinite sleep. Its voice is invariably a shy, kind, or Northern face, all rock; all ice. Let one return at night. Let us gray the meticulous midnight that flees our page. Oh my friends, your hands at seven, a steady beat beneath the wave, and that's all, no more at night. Late afternoon then and the seagull cries so outspoken, these black assortments of sky and beach and sea. All eyes prefer the capture here, sad hearts of inertia. The other side winds through our room, and so we dream again of old Egyptian marble pasted onto the signboard by a gravel road and then we desire the frayed bell-rope that will fall once more, sometime, and travel hastily on its regular glory. The morning sun goes away so swiftly, it rattles many of these barren nights and the unexpected willow. My heart-on-the-carpet others cluster and witness now.

TAPROOT

He can still recall that night, even now as he looks across the water to where a lone tanker begins its slow crawl out to sea. He can remember that little boy who watched a canal man pole his boat along its way. He wonders how that little boy in that distant house became the lanky, weary man that he is now, this man who stands and carefully brushes the seat of his pants and pulls his check blazer close about him as the wind seems to rise at just the moment that he stands, leaves here, and starts for home. He lives in one of those chic apartments etched inside the archaic, cavernous vaults of former warehouses. The carefully placed contents of the rectangular spaces that form his home might yet recall everything he would muzzle. He enters, hangs his check blazer in the closet and goes to the sink and washes his hands. He lights a cigarette and opens a bottle of wine. He takes a glass from a cabinet, some ashes from his cigarette fall into the sink. He pours wine into his glass and walks to his study. He looks briefly at some pictures hung on the wall, turns and looks briefly at some others placed along the outer edge of bookshelves. Now he steps toward his desk. He sits down and looks out the window, out across the water. He closes his eyes for a moment and considers once more those faces locked safe in their frames. He opens his eyes, places his hands upon the keys, and begins to type.

from The Disguise of Events

LET US SUPPOSE

A penny is cheaper than a thought, something animal: a body with four legs, perhaps. A scraped knee, cut and bruised by the architecture, swelled even. And fifty years backwards and under the heel, a cigarette. Its downward spiral and stars so snug in their heavenly design instead. The spit arched over the edge and away. Like that: dwarf zinnias on the other side of the rail and a habitual movement of the foot and under the heel, a cigarette smoldering. So distant from the door, from the animal in its cage, from the outer edge of understanding an image that suggests rather than replicates a car parked surreptitiously in the driveway. Hands in pockets; eyes on the porch and the heel, a cigarette smashed to smithereens, kept at it, gone up in smoke, gone. Twisted and turned, enclosed. Starting out, something less, like the expression: we heard the clock in his voice for the first time today, his hands whistling. Like the expression: line up in front, smoldering — somewhat less than a shock, but more than a surprise. The stairs remain but the guests disappear. Dewy air brightens as a rosy sun rises over stern shoulders and beneath the heel, a cigarette that had glistened. What would soldiers have said if invited to square dance? Too hungry for speaking they stuff their mouths full of macaroni and cheese. Love was like that, too. The manufactories keep producing more hats and more ties and more stickpins and more cigarettes. Professional ones. Ones we've romanticized. Blue one. Plaster of Paris ones. They are wet; they are dried in an endless repetition of stone and air. Storm drain and stop sign: more words only repeat a cage of quotation marks: the animal, the night, the burning march, the temple of grammar, and the inability to move or to think or to spend a dime. Whatever is convenient, lit, cheap, or will rhyme with it. The expression of concern so perfect that prayer enters to glance at a watch, to return an allusion without the utterance. The perfect river: its title lit in matchless color.

GREETING

Something has to appear. A story has no need to begin, only to end. In all of this flux one thing remains: weather. All our shoes have purposes. Choice remains ever out of our control. Something has to appear, after all — something, and we don't know if it'll arrive in a tux or rags, on wing or by flipper and fin. There is no justice, only good subjects.

One remembers a constant lack of resolution, a whole note ever left unfilled. A story has no need to begin only to end so that everyone can go home, so that responses can be netted, lost in the ether outside our windows.

The birds don't care. See what they have done? Today it'll rain yellow towels and unlit cigarettes, says one particularly clever chemistry student.

Nobody tacks dreams to a board outside a room anymore. The room is empty now; the hallway, dark. Look outside at all that weather! Sweet harmony, the bird sings, but no one will believe it.

The stones creep out of the ground and are moss covered. This is no place for an encampment, not in this weather.

I am afraid of our own campfire, of the long nights here under the stars, of the streams that flow down from the hillsides. I am afraid of that number. I am afraid of you and your concert of perceptual faculties.

A mountain lion knows no shyness and if he spoke, he would utter our names and his utterance would be stronger than the force of any engine fashioned by our handicraft. He'd call us home. He'd offer the pendant and the orange and the gum and the high heels. He'd offer us a class in patience and in sitting and in waiting quietly for the passage of time and the bird's shrill whistle.

It is the soft sensation of feathers and the sharp pinch of thorns upon our skin. It is the face that isn't his any longer that greets us. It is the gray chair and the brown room. It is all this weather.

The course turns and then straightens, not by chance but by destiny. It is a fact. It is easier to write of the imagined place than of the actual one. Here the claw, claws and the mouth, mouths curses against us, curses worse than any bite.

There is too much of all of this: too much color and too much noise, too many vibrations and too many colors, too much rustling of feathers and too much whistling of birds, too much weather.

BUMP AND GRIND

This is how we begin: a little paint here, a little dab there. Pointillism is the favored method. All of a sudden our whole canvas takes on shape, all of a sudden it seems to spring to life before our astonished eyes, before the executioner's well-timed swing.

We go off to check on something else but then soon return to argue some more about inclusion and exclusion, the quality of cheap unwanted gifts, tradition and its inescapable lack of variance. We go off to the mountains on weekends in search of butterflies to pin down upon our return home.

What coloring have you got? The policeman asked the bystander at the crossroads. None, officer, this pale and naked manikin replied, unsheathed sword in hand. A child rose up from behind the concrete barrier at the curb, a wind-stuffed leather bag near its foot, grounded. Behind the child, behind the manikin the tall apartment towers ascend skyward, their windows filled with faces puffed up for the ongoing parade, faces that are nothing more than blank forms emptied of language, of national origins. May we propose a day of remembrance, a day of sausages and beer?

On the way to the exhibit the conservator whispered a few unkind words about monuments. My binoculars remained on a shelf high up in a closet on the second floor. His whispers and innuendos made close inspection difficult, criticism of collectibles easy. He was that cruel. It is necessary to forget this trip. It is necessary to forget the conservator's harsh words, almost inaudible but nonetheless distinct and understood. It is necessary to forget the failure, the refusal to exit the cab.

A little bit here, a little bit there: all of this made creative action possible, all of this exists beyond a machine's capabilities and range; all these words, these actions and inactions, these brush strokes. Hasn't this all blended together yet? Step back. Is it still impossible to distinguish the middle of the floor from the edge; the edge from the surrounding wall? Is it still impossible to draw up sides and then when the time is right, when it's safe outside to cross over to the other?

A frail, young woman placed her withered hand on my arm and pulled me farther down the cold dark street. The balloon was in the tree, she said. But the dark, the buildings, the empty field. Vacant, quiet. I didn't see the balloon. I didn't see the child. I only felt my own spine shaking in the unavoidable cold of this irretrievable night.

from Separate Objects

IN THE CENTER OF ALL THINGS

The poet who writes
speaks from the center of
silence.
Silence is not darkness
but is a bright white light.
It is like the bright white
that surrounds the pupil
in the eye of the madman.
It is not the same.
It is not same
because it is un-nameable.
It is that property of
contrariness that seems
impossible.
Incarnate in the poem
it is magical.
Words are wings
on which we fly to meet
in the center of all things.
But how can silence be named?
And what is that bright white
that surrounds this ornament
I wish to speak?

OBJECTS

Handheld

the notebook
as camera

captures
not the world
but the thought

a record
a re / cording of
what
has preceded a
re / chording,
tuning
the instrument

the instrument scrapes
at the surface of language

a vessel
neither full not sailing

object
emptied of all it held
waiting
to be read

SEPARATE OBJECTS

A reflection of *construct*
as a state to be overcome,
obliterated!

Incapable of fulfillment,
short steps from identification
imitate.

The author edges the
seam. The irregular
pattern never written,
detonated.

Imagine:
we're fond of talk,
a precise norm
condemned.

Anticipation washed
beyond insistence
a symbol

that calls attention to
enterprise.

Apprenticeship
closes the last word
regarding difference

an abstract
circle no one

can name
a blind and
certain experience
of miracle.

Yellowed,
the affirmative idea:
to describe and
analyze.

Exact,
like everything.

WHAT'S APPROPRIATE FOR A PAUSE

> *no language is so*
> *copious as to supply words*
> *and phrases for every complex*
> *idea*
> > —James Madison

I think of my work as sculpture.
At least, while I'm writing it.

(inaccuracy is unavoidable)

I think of my work as music.
At least, when I've done writing it.

The shade is drawn.
The shade is still drawn.
I'm coming more and more to think of revision
as expansion.

Words are ideas.
There are some ideas that words cannot express.
Therefore, words are not ideas.

One fortune cookie with two fortunes
that said the same thing.

Something must happen
in order for something to be
anything.

How is poetry different from *writing*?
How is writing different from *poetry*?

(This is a rhymed couplet.)

No models not folded in mine:
definition by example—*disconcerting*
—*red ink showing through white out.*

"I'll write to you again in a week
or so with any further thoughts
I might have or just to let you
know that at that moment I didn't."

That would be a monument!
This, a moment opening to others.
Hyperbole: a lie that does not deceive.

Authority
is its own excuse for being—

Proto-Emersonian:

What a fine day this is!

And the Greek men of the Marathon
Restaurant have stopped dancing for the night.

(Antithesis.)

It's a secret of baffled Zen.
People in "un-education" subtract rules.
It's a secret—to baffle Zen—essential—
in experience most process a secret.

What resumes after the time passes?

An umbrella, a hand, an open book.

"One would not read the book
unless one already understood
it," said one:
And the other:
"it's all genetic."

That his name is Jacob Johnson,
    his mother's name was Dorcus Simons.
That she was a white woman,
    at Accomack, in Virginia.
That Mr. Thomas Kirkly and Doctor Ridgely,
    in Kent and in Dover, know him
That he labored in that country.

Tolerance Integrity Moderation Diligence
Justice Philanthropy Kindness Gentleness

Mercy

Self-help health

The fire that spirit stokes within
Prefer the traditional

Oblivious to the demands of fashion
Propel by continual self-doubt

Prefer the fashionable

Also Thomas Casbon, who saith he
    ran from Lee Master,

at Little Pipe-Creek Furnace,
Maryland.

grab express milestone success
take away one like day
born words report deeds (mis
tenacity laudable remember notable
beat raise sing praise
grab express milestone success
take away one like day

evoked moon named thing described
but what dream is too metaphor completely?

pretension photocopied each one not just
topical versus political Vietnam Apollo-man
word one word more than definition fragrance or law

What's appropriate for a pause?
The leopard has changed his stripes.

A toast use of the page or Black
Mountain etymology for the specific thing
named like the Pope, a phone number

Is that a bad thing?
Will it get me stuck here
for life? Is that my
style? What is style?

My statement regarding your
question is a question and
not a statement. Question

is more important in my work:
more important than what?

I think of my work as sculpture.
At least, while I'm writing it.

I think of my work as music.
At least, when I've done writing it.

(Note: relation between parts is not
necessarily the same thing as narrative.

Different notions create different sounds.
Or should that be "different motions"?

Come on. Let it spin.

ZONDER SUIKER

All of them.

Confused about the date,
the day that it was or
the day that it was becoming.
All of them. Always
looking for two if by land
or three if by sea.
Either way
the red that's in their eyes.
Fire.

Why does the word tart
refer to a sweet?
Why not, say, a rabbit?

Note: the Consulate can
secure every corner
but not shelter a single man.

"G" demonstrates
words' preciousness,
a guttural sound—
each time as if it's
your last breath.

A lot of words
All of them from the outside
A fence
keeping us out
how few of them felt

as from the inside
how few
when there are none
those
such as these
referred to here
say nothing
but shape form and volume
there is nothing to drink
and we are thirsty

In a new speech
when she said
Jane Addams
everyone thought she said
John Adams.

"Democracy like any
other of the living faiths
of men, is so
essentially mystical
that it continually
demands new formulation."

I don't like to shout

across chasms

never mind

rooms.

You dressed a TV

ignoring your normal
vocabulary. Even the
word "cassettes" is
repeated for a second
time. You want the
practice to make
communication easy and
the equivalent of important
address. The words and
phrases will stamp you
as charming. Admire
buildings. Beg their
pardon by saying,
Pardon.

The outbreak. The intake.
The fumes. Not perfume.
The center. The periphery.
The correct. Not the false.
Sea gull. Car. Light.
Water. Brick. Cement.
Road. Street. Intersection
Store. Window. Door.
Furniture. Bottles. Papers.
People. Ducks. Birds.
Tree. Roof. Sky. Plane.
Window. Smoke-stack.
Blinds. Curtains. Shutters.
Steps. Lights. Desks.
Offices. Houses. Stores.
Windows. Doors. People.

"In Amsterdam,

the head has taken over
and the heart has
almost disappeared."

I thought you would
kiss my hand,
but instead you
scratched your nose.

Maybe smell is
the central fact
of who we are.

A week ago
we saw
Livingstone's
grave.

Stanley
was nowhere
to be
found. You

hear?

This word means
only one thing.
Nothing will be
allowed to mean
anything until
this word means
only one thing.

I have my doubts.
Few bricks.

The city cries out:
Come out! Come out!

We sit in in in
the house. Insistent
in our ways
against its. The city
cries; we plug up
our ears.

Our ears, our ears
—have wings.

A primary today

and a slogan

Don't Bite The Hand That Beats You

Re-Elect The President

and tomorrow

Remarkable flowers
lift themselves
up in the morning
in the sun
they sweat
and their smell is so
sweet

What a map!

These fact
have no signs
And these signs
point everywhere

The door opened.
The hogs ran outside.
The boys came back.
The big dog had the
   little dog in its mouth.
The dogs came back inside.
The big dog spit the little
   dog out.
The little dog could speak.

When an *e* is added
to *goed*, the *d* is
pronounced as a
Dutch *j* which is
sort of like an
English *y*.

How come?

Weet ik veel?
How do I know?

The high school dropout

rate in Baltimore is 50%.

disarray and poverty

glamour and energy

A whirlwind a snowball a take off

a Great Barbecue

Can you tell me
when White House press secretary
Marlin Fitzwater said that
"the forces of repression,
suppression and anarchy
cannot be allowed to continue"
was he referring to the
White House?

Tick-tock,
look at the clock.
Go now,
"to be there
where it is."

Oregon and Texas
are yet unsung

look outside

It's Amsterdam!

There's a canal in my eye.

so many faith

museums
each one of them
in their silence and emptiness
thriving

let's get together
and express our
"holy anger"

We make the weapons
with which you enslave us.

The new system.

We pay the taxes
with which you imprison us.

The new system.

In the textile industry
70% lost their jobs.
In the colleges
30% lost their jobs.
So, you see,
they are doing very well
in the new system.

This is a necessity
we just have to accept.

If you saw images of
Christ every day, how could you
not believe in Christ?

And now—
how can anyone
not believe in buying
and selling?

A student from Dresden:

"Now there are fewer friendships,
but more interests. Money, cars,
people without power.
A candle going out.
Our revolution dying."

Curious,
even the photographs we took
turned out very dark.

We have three windows
that overlook a canal.
Everything has worked
out well.

all talk there, wherever uttered,
having the pitch of a call

across the water

James put to another
direction

which will be heard?

memory

round and circular
it remains
after all else
it pulls back in
and remains
round and circular

memory

Questions become exclamations
America, a remembered Europe

The glasswort community turns
into a salt-marsh grass community.

L.A. into Den Hague

Rubles into Deutsche Marks

X into Y

and Z

back into the land

Remarkable: both
spoonbill and eider

breed here in the same area.

Sometimes their nests are in fact

within the same square meter.

Well, screw my face up
and push my glasses down

it's a wire from Fitzwater.
This time: "without fear
of infamy."

Paring knife

"Justice will prevail"
—President George Bush

Executive order
from two to seven days
—Governor Pete Wilson

Armor-plated kindness

that piece of the pie
too small to either
stand or stamp upon

without destroying your toes.

smoked meat
flesh
the sign meant
fresh
luxury
new vice
either way

accompanied
        after Herbert

a company
a compact

a compass
missing

i.e. the famous "Three Acorns"

The roadside was littered
with inspiration.

The poem
was one way to curb it.

Did you know that
the same year
Stevens
died Dickinson's *Collected*
Poems were published
for the first time and
the McDonald's Corporation
began?

Why, why are you
telling us this?
Shouldn't we be
discussing new ideas
of order?

In order to have a message
is it necessary to have an answer?
Why not just a question?
Accidents are more interesting
than accuracies.
To say—briefly—something
somewhere. An invitation
more than anything else here.

In his poem "Resignation"
Longfellow calls life on Earth
"a suburb of the life elysian."

There is no need to go
beyond America to find
alternatives to America.

I'm trying to stand in
it not for or against it.

One page to be filled
and be held accountable
for it.

It's the last time we're going to be
on the train past the new bridge in Rotterdam.

A view, an object,
or good food at a restaurant

Shakespeare and Cervantes
died in the same year

A walk along the dunes
west of Haarlem

Every morning the flagstones
were strewn with sand,
sometimes in patterns.

People get up to go
to the bathroom. I have already
gone. I was the first to go.
Again, I was the first.
What is next?

I haven't finished my wine
and already the coffee.

"Zonder suiker, alstublieft."

"Error, crime and adultery:
that's all that makes men
interesting."—Raymond Queneau

over Newfoundland
perhaps

"Error, crime, and adultery"

DRUMS

The Cup
What holds the air of any expression?
Emptied, it says the following to me
on Wednesday: you are full of it.

White Paper
Lines man! He said. Like, they are
horizontal. I hear you. So what
will become of the paper? Eat it.

The Rug
"The Murders in the Rue Morgue." Not
there, but the spilt blood of those murdered
texts lapped in ceaseless waves at my feet.

Watch
What you hear is the flux of tense:
is/was, are/were, etc. Well, how about
it? What tense are you: then/now?

Wood Door
Pulled tooth. My floor has blood and
blood has sharp edges. It's like this: finished
when the right hand has the left hand tied.

The Clock
Smile. Your face moves me from point
A to point B. I've tried to stop you/
me, but I only bumped crudely into myself.

Stone Hallway

This house has sky to frame its every branch,
all that pattern held in just so. This
has been the story of rivers, oceans, and fenders.

from Unfold the Mid-Point Now

WHAT HE THINKS

Adorn him with flowers
and lead him out of the city.
He tortures himself with needless labor
and gives pains to his readers.
He enlists verbs in his service
and shouts "henceforth!"
He is a disturbance.
He is the gnat that sticks in the eye of Usura.
He would be the whole parade
and have us teach his gospel.
He has betrayed us, coins jingle in his lines.
He may try to save us with hollow
words such as "halo."
Send him then, with flowers,
out of the city. In the desert,
let him struggle for life.
In the desert, let him struggle
to get more out of language.
"Thirst," he says and a snake shakes his hand.
He remembers,
happy hours of childhood, of
youth before the interruptions
of the infinitive "to write."
His flowers wilt.
His hands follow his flowers.
They burn in the sun as his books
burn in the city. "Henceforth,"
he'll shout no more. His ashes
blow as lyres unto the city.
His chords, dark ashes, blacken the streets.
Through cracks, his ashes whisper "therefore."
This is what he thinks.

WHEN I THINK OF RICHARD

I first met Richard
    And I said
"Cats walk on little cat feet.
    What about this word *through*?"
This was about the time he got involved with his first wife.
    Was no better than a...
Richard was like someone who had
    A circle of people led by
An editor I was always waiting for
    There was a small public
He walked up to me
    Richard had an uncanny gift
And he saved everything
    Richard was very happy
He'd tell them, "Fuck off!"
    He just left without explaining himself.
The only thing I remember is that
    Vonnegut just mentioned his name to me the other day.
People would ask him to read
    The irony is that
Richard read a contract
    When *Trout Fishing* hit
It set off an echo all over the English-speaking world
    The parade was for Moloch
He joined the parade
    We'd go to the Palm for dinner and have those huge lobsters
He was miserable.

Before he was rich
    He was very much against any kind of social classes
He never talked
    Richard wasn't very political

At the time, I suggested that people read Shelley
     He was always conservative, though
After he first made it big
     Richard would talk
I saw Richard several times
     I remember one summer
Richard was set on being the
     "Image of a body"
Roughly he was conscious that
     He was suspicious
Living in Bolinas
     He was uncomfortable
Then all of a sudden
     He viewed himself
"No, it's not possible"
     All these public figures
Attractiveness
     Three fifths a day, two fifths of whiskey
A cowboy atmosphere
     There was no pattern
I was startled
     He'd tell a story
A lot of people have said that
     Although he wasn't the type

The first time he had a real home
     He was sober
I can't say why
     Richard destroyed the relationship
He was very used up and overrun
     We were
What was left?
     The more legitimate

Ran the show
	Bellow, Mailer, Roth, Updike, Malamud
I was around him
	And she came to live with him
Richard was in love
	He was read by
A hyena in American literature
	I saw it as a little
Silly
	He wasn't read by intellectuals
Of all my writing
	Which got a lot of audience
Richard had a fascination with
	The woman on the jacket
He didn't have a kind of naivete
	He once called us from
Europe or Tokyo and
	Because he got attached to his alcoholism
He wanted to write, though
	But he also said
"A beautiful place
	What am I doing here?"
"You're destroying our work."
	He had given up drinking for
I would come put him to bed
	And I talked to him
About self-pity and middle-age

However beautiful the place is
	A dollar's worth of trouble with
This he had taped
	The suicide
He was in a box and said

Returned from Tokyo in the spring
The trouble
    Even if I'd known
Yet I knew
    Know how to handle money
Crazy jokes
    Half of the $600
Couldn't
    You've got to do
In day to day matters
    I listened patiently and then he said
How he might just take
    Sort of calculated
You'll receive instruction
    I hadn't
Now that I look back
    Thirty years
People were out to get him
    Amsterdam, Tokyo, or Berlin
Some of the stuff I took to the neighbors
    I saw him
He called me
    At the end of May
Then he went out to Bolinas
    I think he decided he was
And I know he
    As it turned out
The house
    Would still be there

from The Territory of Innocence

MAKE OF THIS LIFE, A NOTEBOOK (*Excerpt*)

Left the reader floating in the white space
of a near empty page and there by the left
hand margin was the word   "yes"
I thought it was inscribed to me
from you telling me   what?
We were through or I love you
I thought: what does it mean?
Who wrote it? The page
was then turned by a familiar hand.
And then I knew, yes? The turned page was
opulent, was abundant—
rich in imported rosewoods, in-
laid with brass work known to all as buhl
work. The turner's hands
turned again and again, spun the wheel
which the text had become,
bound by a spoke heart laced and ever
turning just as the pages turned.
Rapid and rich and ever growing: a folio
an octavo, a duodecimo until black
appeared upon black and what happened and
what was happening became unclear. When
was what and what was when? Beyond
reason; beyond memory for a moment all
turned white again
and there in the textured folds of an opaque
stock we glimpsed ourselves reading this
and writing more, together, yet
kept separate by the words we wrote.
Startlingly, there was no longer a reflection
in this printed mirror. We had

become an unreasoned one.

*

"OVER THE PREDICTABLE BEAT"
I'm trying to read the next line,
but from across the street
comes the disturbance of an electric
guitar's twang:
There is no predictable beat.

WHY'S (*Excerpt*)

Somewhere
on the far side of
the distant place
is this mirror
image of
what is
already known.
We see it here,
but strive to reach it
there.
Where all is
harmony;
here is discord.
We build on it
a symphony of regret.
Forgiven,
the wanderer nonetheless
travels
to unravel
the double strand
of what we are.
Still,
light off this
mirror
distracts or
refracts
us. From
the source in
to the mouth of
— what I was
saying. What

was I saying?
"Somewhere."

*

free
already
to
become
one
part of
what he
already
is
turning
in-
to one
al-
ready and
free

from The House of Land

one must be
that is
one must be
curious

We killed a rattlesnake there,
so we called it Rattlesnake Hill.

And then we looked at Eliot and
Milton for the meaning of suffering.

We killed...
and then...

We remembered Vaucanson had exhibited
his duck in 1741.

I mean...

the house,
about the house

(Guilt)

Does anyone anything?

Story of a man
who wins the lottery,
but is hit by a car.

(Paranoia)

What is motive?

bath of word
head bowed
bathe in
clear sign
Protestant rearing
any town

two
asleep in each
room has
order, perfection
too good to
breed im-
perfection.

A pebble wobbles

Who introduced Wright
to Wang Wei and Morris?
Do our parents have enough
to eat, adequate clothes,
a splendid view?

The I must leave
the mind.

POPULARITY

Complexity of motive

We killed a rattlesnake there,
so we called it Rattlesnake Hill.

Acknowledgments

Thanks to the editors of the journals where some of the new poems have been published and to the publishers of the books and chapbooks wherein all the other poems have appeared.

Eunoia Review: "Romance"
October Hill Magazine: "Lights Left On"
Posit: "Double or Nothing," "Pond and Ocean," and "Work"
Verse-Virtual: "Backwards," "Everything Silent," and "Wishful Thinking"
The Worcester Review: "Thoroughfare"

After Math. Cyber Wit, 2023.
A Field Guide to the Rehearsal. Blaze Vox, 2022.
Frame Narrative. Blaze Vox, 2018.
sound / hammer. Quale, 2015.
Parallel Lines. Shearsman, 2011.
The Walls of Circumstance. Avec, 2004.
The Disguise of Events. Quale, 2002.
Separate Objects. Left Hand, 1998.
Unfold the Mid-Point Now. Open Township, 1988.
The Territory of Innocence. Writers Forum, 1987.
The House of Land. Spectacular Diseases, 1986.

www.ingramcontent.com/pod-product-compliance
Lightning Source LLC
Chambersburg PA
CBHW022008080426
42733CB00007B/531